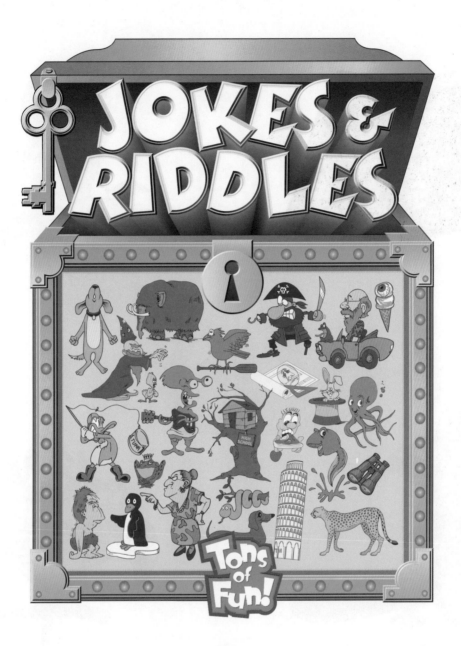

JOKES & RIDDLES

Tons of Fun!

By
Chris Tait

Visit us at **www.kidsbooks.com**

INTRODUCTION

What's funnier than a chicken crossing the road? How about a polar bear riding a bike?

Turn the page for the most hilarious jokes and riddles around. There are tons of knock-knock knee slappers, silly school jokes, awesome animal jokes, and much, much more. So what are you waiting for? Get ready for some side-splitting laughter with your friends and family!

XTREME-LY FUNNY

Why don't snowboarders make good plumbers?

Because they only know about half-pipes!

What do you call the biggest skateboarder in the world?

Ollie-phant!

Why are skateboarders so cheap about buying clothes?

Because they believe in free style!

Why did the extreme surfer think that the sea was his friend?

Because it gave him a big wave as he went by!

Knock, knock!
Who's there?
Caddy!
Caddy who?
Caddy ya own surfboard, dude!

What is a bungee jumper's favorite part of a song?

The bridge!

What is a snowboarder's favorite type of vegetation?

The hand plant!

How do snowboarders face a hill?

Nose first!

What did the gloomy snowboarder say when he got off the lift?

"It's all downhill from here!"

Why are in-line skaters so excited?

Because they never feel board!

What did the boarders call the girl who loved to do 360s?

Mary-Go-Round!

What did the extreme biker call her winter wheels?

Her ice cycle!

Why did the skydiver feel a little nervous during her jump?

Because she had a sinking feeling!

What advice did the white-water kayaker give as he went over the rapid?

"Roll with it!"

Why did the skateboarder pick up speed going downhill?

Because he had an inclination to go faster!

What do you call the guy who is the world's best on the half-pipe?

The chairman of the board!

KNOCK, KNOCK!

Knock, knock!
Who's there?
Ben!
Ben Who?
Ben a long time since I've seen you!

Knock, knock!
Who's there?
Don!
Don who?
Don tell me you don't remember me!

Knock, knock!
Who's there?
Ax!
Ax who?
Ax nicely, and I might tell you!

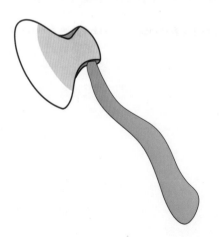

Knock, knock!
Who's there?
House!
House who?
House about you let me come inside?

Knock, knock!
Who's there?
Arnold!
Arnold who?
Arnold friend from far away!

Knock, knock!
Who's there?
Isaiah!
Isaiah who?
Isaiah nothing else until you let me in!

Knock, knock!
Who's there?
Osborn!
Osborn who?
Osborn today!
That makes it my birthday!

Knock, knock!
Who's there?
Chester!
Chester who?
Chester luck, you forgot
my name again!

Knock, knock!
Who's there?
Betty!
Betty who?
Betty doesn't even know
his own name!

Knock, knock!
Who's there?
Chuck!
Chuck who?
Chuck and see if you
recognize me!

Knock, knock!
Who's there?
Leggo!
Leggo who?
Leggo of me and I'll tell you!

Knock, knock!
Who's there?
Sultan!
Sultan who?
Sultan pepper makes everything
taste better!

RUBBER CHICKEN JOKES

Who tells the best rubber chicken jokes?

Comedi-HENS!

How does a rubber chicken send mail?

In a HEN-velope!

What do you get when you cross a rubber chicken with a cow?

ROOST beef!

Why did the rubber chicken cross the playground?

To get to the other SLIDE!

What do you get when you cross a rubber chicken with a cement mixer?

A bricklayer!

What do rubber chickens grow on?

Eggplants!

Why did the rubber chicken cross the road?
To get to the RUBBER side!
Why did the gum cross the road?
It was stuck to the chicken's foot!

Why did the turkey cross the road?

To prove he wasn't a chicken!

Why do rubber chickens make great basketball players?

Because they always bounce back in the fourth quarter!

Why is a fish easier to weigh than a rubber chicken?

Fish come with their own scales!

Why did the rubber chicken cross the basketball court?

He heard the referee calling FOWLS!

How does a rubber chicken make cake?

From scratch!

How did the rubber chicken learn to lay eggs?

The farmer showed him an EGG-xample!

Why couldn't the rubber chicken fly through the window?

It was closed!

When is the best time to buy rubber chicks?

When they're going CHEEP!

Why do rubber chickens lay eggs?

Because if they just dropped them, they'd break!

SILLY JOKES

What goes zzub, zzub, zzub?

A bee flying backward!

How do you catch monkeys?

Hang from a tree and make a noise like a banana!

Why can you dive from 300 feet right into a soda pop without hurting yourself?

Because it is a soft drink!

What happens when you cross an ape man with a tiger?

You get Tarzan stripes forever!

What do you use to cut through giant waves?

A sea saw!

Where do frogs leave their hats?

In a croakroom!

What do you get from nervous cows?

Milk shakes!

What do the animals read in zoos?

Gnuspapers!

What do you call pigs that write letters?

Pen pals!

What is green, curly, and plays pop music?

A transistor lettuce!

Which fish wears spurs and a cowboy hat?

Billy the Cod!

How would you describe a wild party at a camping site?

Intense (in tents) excitement!

Why didn't the two worms go into Noah's ark in an apple?

Because everyone had to go in pears!

What did the bull sing to the cow?

"When I fall in love, it will be for heifer."

Heard about the exhausted kangaroo?

He was out of bounds!

Wacky Wizardry

What do math wizards say when they lift a curse?

"Hex-a-gone!"

What did the wizard say when he couldn't find his wife?

"Witch way did she go?"

If three ghosts run a race, which ghost will win?

The one with the most spirit!

What does a wizard's cat like just before it goes to bed?

A sorcerer of milk!

What did the wizard say when he met the witch he was going to marry?

"So, this is the bride and broom!"

What does the wizard's sister eat when she goes to the beach?

Sand-witches!

What did the wizard's wife say when he changed her into a bird?

"Owl fly away!"

What is the favorite name for werewolves?

Harry! (hairy)

What is the wizard's favorite soap opera called?

All My Cauldrons!

What did the witch say to the monster that ate too fast?

"Wow, you really are a-gobblin'!"

How does a wizard keep his potions safe from burglars?

With a warlock!

What does a wizard say when he wants the lights to go on?

"Abra-candelabra!"

Where do wizards go to test their skill?

Spelling bees!

Why are wizards so good in fishing school?

Because they really know how to cast a spell!

When the wizard found his friend, what had she been doing?

Witch-hiking!

What did the wizard tell his wife after he tried to change her into a bird?

I've got some bat news . . . !

 ILLY SPIES

How do spies send secret messages in a forest?

By moss code!

What happened when the spy slept under the car?

She woke up oily the next morning!

What is a silly secret agent's favorite movie?

Spy Hard!

Why do gophers make good spies?

Because they know how to dig for dirt!

What is a junior secret agent's favorite movie?

Spy Kids!

Where do sick spies go?

The ho-spy-tal!

Why did the secret agent cross the road?

To catch the other spy!

What do you call it when one cow spies on another?

A steak-out!

What is a spy's favorite TV show?

Hidden Camera!

How did the spy feel when he spilled fruit punch on himself?

Like he'd been caught red-handed!

What do double-crossing spies do on vacation?

They lie around!

Why do informers smell so bad?

Because they're always spilling the beans!

What did the secret agent give the suspicious double-crossing spy?

A lie-defector test!

Why do mummies make good spies?

Because they are good at keeping things under wraps!

CAFETERIA COMEDY

What soup is fresh in the cafeteria but still boring?

Chicken new-dull!

What do little kids get at the cafeteria in the afternoon?

A nap-snack!
(knapsack)

Here's a cafeteria recipe: Throw out the outside, cook the inside, eat the outside, throw out the inside. What's it for?

An ear of corn!

Why did the cook bake bread for the cafeteria?

Because he kneaded the dough!

What is the worst-tasting drink in the cafeteria?

Nas-tea!

Where does the cook shop for vegetables?

The stalk market!

How did the cup and saucer feel about the shoddy way they had been washed?

They thought it was dish-picable!

What dessert should you always eat sitting down?

Chair-ee pie!

What did the potatoes say
after the big vote?

"The eyes have it!"

What makes the cook sadder
the skinnier it gets?

An onion!

What do you call someone who works
in the cafeteria fixing fruit?

A peach cobbler!

How do school inspectors
like their eggs?

Hard-boiled!

What do you call it when you can't
have dessert until after lunch?

Choco-late!

UNDER WHERE?

Knock, knock!
Who's there?
Irish.
Irish who?
Irish my underwear wasn't showing!

What did the pair of underwear say when it was making a toast?

"Bottoms up!"

What did the man say when he took out his thermal underwear for the winter?

"Long time, no seam!"

What did the woman do with her silky underwear?

She satin them!

Why are boxer shorts so sad?

Because they feel under-appreciated!

What kind of dessert can you eat in your underwear?

Shortbread!

What did the army shorts say to the boxer shorts?

"Brief me!"

What kind of briefs do cows wear?

Udderwear!

What kind of briefs does Thor wear?

Thunderpants!

What do you feel when you have to throw out an old pair of underwear?

Brief grief!

Why was the musician so embarrassed when his shorts fell down?

Because he thought the band had let him down!

What did the tank top say to the pair of long underwear?

"Let's keep this brief!"

What did the long underwear say to the tank top?

"Don't be short with me!"

What did the silk underwear say to the cotton briefs?

"Slip around, you might learn something!"

What did the cotton briefs say to the silk underwear?

"Man, you're smooth!"

What kind of boxer shorts do supervillains wear?

Underworld underwear!

COMIC CRITTERS

Why did the cat sing all morning long?

He had tune-a-fish for breakfast!

What do you get from an Arctic cow?

Cold cream!

What do you use to count cows?

A cow-culator!

What do you give a sick pig?

Oink-ment!

What did the owl think when he lost his voice?

He didn't give a hoot!

Why do geese fly south for the winter?

It's too far to walk!

What do you call a sleeping bull?

A bulldozer!

What kind of bird is always
out of breath?

A puffin!

Why do fish live in salt water?

*Because pepper makes
them sneeze!*

What do you get when you cross
two elephants with a fish?

Swimming trunks!

Why are fish the smartest animals?

*They spend all their time
in a school!*

Why did the farmer name his
pig "Ink?"

*Because it kept running
out of the pen!*

Why did the cow cross the road?

To get to the udder side!

If apes live in trees, where
do they sleep?

In apricots!

Why are bison such good musicians?

They have fantastic horns!

CLASSROOM Crack-ups

What did the boy say when he had to clean the blackboards after class?

"I chalked it up to experience!"

What did the girl say when asked how her history class was?

"It's old hat!"

How long does history class feel?

"Four score and seven years . . ."

Why did the girl think that she was in charge of the class?

Because she had the ruler!

Why did the student mail a clock to his science class?

He wanted to see time travel!

What do you call a boy who excels in phys. ed.?

Jim! (gym)

What do you call a student who misses Spanish, French, and English classes?

Truant in three languages!

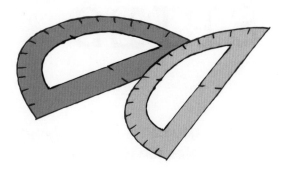

Why does math class feel so long?

It must be the protractors!

What did the boy who wanted to stay home say when asked where he didn't feel well?

"In school, mostly!"

What did the girl say when asked why she didn't like going to school?

"Oh, I like going. I just don't like getting there!"

Why did the student think that she could make toast in science class?

She heard that they'd be using bun-sun burners!
(Bunsen burners)

What is the best thing to eat in math class?

Pi!

What do you call the last day of school?

The first day of the year!

How do you know that you've been staring at the chalk too long?

When you get really board!

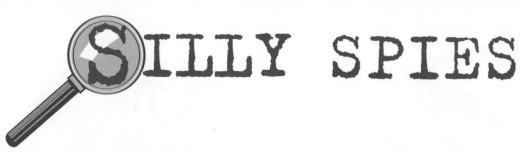

SILLY SPIES

What do you call a secret agent with great vision?

An eye spy!

Why did the spy spend the day in bed?

Because he was told to stay undercover!

What game do young spies learn on the playground?

Hide-and-seek!

What kind of food do super-sleuths love?

Spy-see food!

What is a secret agent's favorite car game?

I Spy!

What do you call a secret agent who spies for both sides?

Double trouble!

Why was Quasimodo such a good secret agent?

Because he always had a hunch!

What kind of shoes do athletic spies wear?

Sneak-ers!

Why did the spy think that something was wrong?

Because she had a sneaking suspicion!

How did the spy pass a test in spy school?

He cheated without getting caught!

What does the British Secret Service call its yellow-haired spy?

James Blond!

Why should you never play hide-and-seek with spies?

Because they always sneak a peek!

What is a spy's favorite dessert?

S-pie!

Why did the spy think that the floor had lips?

Because she knew that the walls had ears!

HOCKEY PUCKS AND YUCKS

Every time Bob and Steve played hockey in Steve's driveway, Steve's dog would jump up and start biting Bob's leg.

One day, Bob asked Steve, "Is your dog trying to protect you from me?"

"No," replied Steve. "He just doesn't like hockey."

"He doesn't?" asked Bob. "How come?"

"Because," answered Steve. *"He's a boxer."*

Why didn't the puck go to jail?

Because the goalie saved him!

Fred: **Did you hear about the center who stepped out of the shower soaking wet and turned on the light?**
Jill: **No, what happened?**
Fred: *He took a penalty shock!*

Jill: **Did you hear about the two players who were in the NHL even though they were only 15?**
Fred: **No, what happened?**
Jill: *When the league found out, they got a double minor!*

Why was Cinderella's hockey team so bad?

She had a pumpkin for a coach!

What happened when the hockey player told a joke?

The ice cracked up!

What happened at the tie game when the ice melted?

The game went into sodden-depth overtime!

Why do the Halifax Hens have such bad uniforms?

Because they're cheep!

What is the hockey player's favorite part of cake?

The ICING, of course!

What do you get when you cross hockey skates with a bicycle?

An ice-cycle!

What part of a hockey arena is never the same?

The changing rooms!

Why are hockey players such bad dancers?

They're afraid of getting holding penalties!

How are defensemen like dentists?

They both take out teeth when they go to work.

UNDER WHERE?

How did the boxer feel when he ran out of underpants?

Short-tempered!

What kind of underwear works best for small dogs?

Boxer shorts, of course!

Knock, knock!
Who's there?
Lucy!
Lucy who?
Lucy lastic will make your underwear fall down!

What did the man say when he took off his too-tight underwear?

"That's a brief relief!"

Did you read the book about the history of underwear?

Yes, but I thought it was a little brief!

What do you call your evening underwear?

Late bloomers!

What do you see under there?

Underwear?

What do you call instructions for underwear?

The brief brief!

Why does underwear hate these kinds of books?

Because it's always the butt of the joke!

What did the boxer shorts say to the socks that were drying on the line?

"You hang out here often?"

What part of the military handles the underwear?

The rear admiralty!

Knock, knock!
Who's there?
Nunya!
Nunya who?
Nunya business what kind of boxer shorts I'm wearing!

What advice do you give to a contortionist about his underwear?

Don't get your shorts in a knot!

What did the man call the full-body underwear that he lost?

His long-gones!

How can your friends help you with your underwear in a pinch?

With a wedgie!

What do you call a man who forgets to put on his underpants?

Nicholas! (knicker-less)

XTREME-LY FUNNY

Why don't they build skate parks in outer space?

Because you can't get any air there!

What did the BMXer say when she crashed into the straw?

"I guess it's time to hit the hay!"

What do pro skateboarders love about their jobs?

The everyday grind!

What do you call a surfer who only wants to board in Rio?

Brazil nuts!

Knock, knock!
Who's there?
Canoe!
Canoe who?
Canoe help me wax my surfboard?

What do you call the best extreme skier?

Snow Wonder!

What do snowboarders do when they have an itch?

Pull a backscratcher!

What do BMXers love to do around Easter?

Bunny hops!

What happened when the BMXer landed the giant jump?

She got a big shock!

What do boarders love to do in public, even though it's bad manners?

The nosepick!

Why did the boarder think she could fly?

Because she was wearing her airwalks!

Why don't Aussies get sleepy on the waves?

Because they're all wake boarding!

Why is in-line trick skating like flying a plane?

Because all anyone remembers is the landing!

What do you say when an extreme rock climber almost falls?

"Get a grip!"

What did the boarder's friend say when she saw him wipe out?

"Looks like he's going to get that much-needed break!"

Why couldn't the silly man use his new water skis?

He was searching for a lake with a slope!

COMIC CRITTERS

What is the most up-to-date animal in the zoo?

The gnu, of course!

What did the man say when he heard the story about the giraffe's hindquarters?

"Now that's a tall tail!"

Why are leopards easier to see than jaguars?

Because you can spot a leopard!

What kind of book is *Black Beauty*?

A pony tale!

What did the cheetah say when it was accused?

"You've gotta believe me! I'm not lion!"

Which big cat can you never trust?

The cheetah! (cheater)

What winged creature is the most sarcastic?

The mockingbird!

What type of bird is the most enthusiastic?

The ravin'!

What do housekeeper rodents do?

Mousework!

What did the antelope say when it read the paper?

"That's gnus to me!"

What school subject do snakes like best?

Hissssstory, of course!

What do frogs like best about vacationing in the tropics?

The croak-o-nuts!

What kind of shoes do frogs wear on vacation?

Open-toad sandals!

What do you call a snake that leads an orchestra?

A boa conductor!

SILLY JOKES

What is the most common illness among spies?

A code in the nose!

Who is Tibetan, hairy, and courageous?

Yak the Giant Hero!

What would you get if motorists were only allowed to drive pink minis?

A pink car nation!

Where do farmers leave their pigs when they go into town?

At porking meters!

Hear about the dancer who became a spy?

Her phone was tapped!

Who takes Christmas presents to police stations?

Santa Clues!

What is gray and has four legs and a trunk?

A mouse going on a holiday!

If buttercups are yellow, what color are hiccups?

Burple!

What builds nests down in pits?

Mynah (miner) birds!

Why do cows wear bells?

Because their horns don't work!

What do fish in the South Pacific sing?

"Salmon-chanted Evening"

What do you call an elf
that lives with your granny?

An old folk's gnome!

What goes "Woof woof, tick tick"?

A watch dog!

What is green, curly, and religious?

Lettuce pray!

Where do astronauts
leave their space ships?

At parking meteors!

Wacky Wizardry

What do you call a wizard who tells the weather?

A forecaster!

What did the wizard name his daughter?

Wand-a!

Why do wizards need housekeepers?

To take care of the magic dust!

Why did the witch's children do so well in school?

Because they were wiz kids!

What do you call a phony wizard?

A magi-sham!

What do you call a wizard with basic good manners?

Simply charming!

Are all wizards good?

Not hex-actly!

What do the young wizards call their oldest teacher?

Tyrannosaurus hex!

What did the little wizard say when his first spell worked?

"Hexellent!"

Why don't single wizards dance?

Because they don't have ghoul-friends!

What did the little wizards call their baseball team?

The Bat News Bears!

What's a wizard's favorite subject in school?

Spelling!

Why didn't the wizard predict the future for a living?

There was no prophet in it!

What kind of jewelry do wizards wear?

Charm bracelets!

Where do young wizards go to learn?

Charm school!

How many wizards does it take to change a lightbulb?

None. Wizards don't need to use lightbulbs!

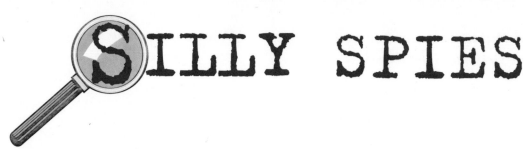

SILLY SPIES

What do spies give each other when they get married?

Decoder rings!

What did the American spy say when he had the proof?

"C I A-in't lying!"

Why did the spy handbook seem so empty?

Because it was written in invisible ink!

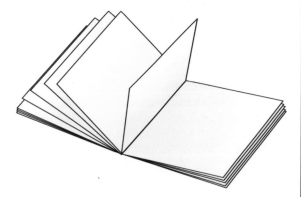

Who is a secret agent's favorite superhero?

Spy-derman!

What did the supervillain say to the spy?

"It isn't easy being mean!"

Who did the secret agent's reckless driver work for?

The Secret Swerve-ice!

Why did the spy say, "Keep your ear to the ground?"

Because he was listening for his shoe phone to ring!

What did the detective say to the handy spy?

"You're crafty!"

What villain is the most disagreeable?

Dr. No!

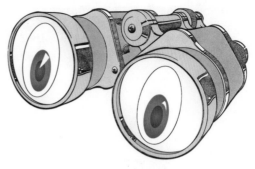

What does an undercover optometrist sell?

Spyglasses!

What do you call two spies in a diner?

Counter-espionage!

What do spies use to open secret doors?

A snea-key!

Why did the spy dig a hole in her backyard?

To hide her trench coat!

What did the spy discover about the laundered money?

It was a cover-up!

CAFETERIA COMEDY

Why did the student start a food fight with his meat loaf?

The only other option was to eat it!

What stops a cafeteria food fight?

A peas treaty!

What did the utensil say when the spoon asked what he was spooning?

"Try and fork-get about it!"

Why did the student not want to eat his mystery meat?

He wanted to have teeth left for dessert!

What do you call a cook at the cafeteria?

The torture king!

Why is the cook so funny at the cafeteria?

Because she'll have your stomach in knots!

What do you call someone who eats every bit of his cafeteria lunch?

A masochist!

When the cook was very angry, what did she do?

She whipped the cream!

Who loves the school cafeteria food?

My pet goat. But it also ate one of my shoes and a tin can for breakfast!

What is the one good reason to eat everything on your plate at the cafeteria today?

So it won't end up as leftovers tomorrow!

What do you call someone who volunteers to eat lunch at the school cafeteria?

Starving!

When is it okay to eat at a cafeteria?

When it is your last meal!

What does the sign over the cafeteria entrance say?

"Abandon all hope, ye who enter here!"

Why was the cook so mean to eggs?

He loved to beat them!

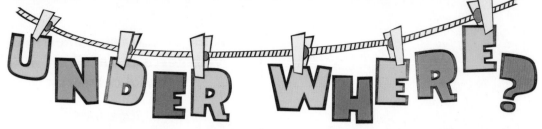

UNDER WHERE?

What do you call a telephone receptionist who wears silk boxer shorts?

A smooth operator!

What do you call bleached briefs that shrink in the wash?

Whitey tighties!

What kind of underwear do sheep wear?

Baaaaaxer shorts!

What do elephants wear to the beach?

Their swim trunks!

What kind of underwear do gardeners wear?

Bloomers!

What secrets do you hear about underwear?

Bloomer rumors!

What do you call scratchy woollen underwear?

Itchy britches!

What famous bear needs to wear diapers?

Winnie the Pooh!

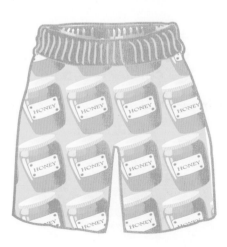

What did the sign over the underwear store say?

"Get your butt in here!"

What does someone who makes underwear do?

He stitches britches!

Why did Santa need new underwear?

Because his were full of ho-ho-holes!

What did the nice woman say to the man in his swimming trunks?

"Those really suit you!"

Knock, knock!
Who's there?
Ican!
Ican who?
Ican see your underwear!

What did the vacationer say when he got too much sand in his swimsuit?

"I think I overpacked my trunks!"

What do you call someone who steals underwear from babies?

A diaper swiper!

XTREME-LY FUNNY

What did the experienced surfer say about the youngster who got stranded?

"Paddle teach him!"

Why do boarders love Thanksgiving?

It's a good chance to practice their carving!

What did the surfer think of the wave in front of him?

He thought it was swell!

Knock, knock!
Who's there?
Wanda!
Wanda who?
Wanda teach me how to snowboard?

What kind of music do surfers like best?

New wave, of course!

What dance do boarders go to every winter?

The Snowball!

Why do bikers get upset when they have to do the dishes?

Because they worry about their forks all the time!

What does a BMXer call his posse?

The Chain Gang!

What do you call a silly climber suspended on a rock face?

Dope on a rope!

What do you call a climber scrambling to keep her grip on the mountain?

Grope on a rope!

What do you call a climbing line hanging over a cliff?

Rope on a slope!

How did the climber get to the top of the mountain before everyone else?

He sneaked a peak!

Do most climbers think that they will fall?

Knot if they can help it!

What do climbers and plastic wrap have in common?

They both know how to cling on!

Why don't skydivers like portable phones?

Because they don't believe in going cordless!

What did the skydiver say when her pack didn't open?

"Chute!"

KNOCK, KNOCK!

Knock, knock!
Who's there?
Gino!
Gino who?
Gino who it is. I'm your twin brother!

Knock, knock!
Who's there?
Phil!
Phil who?
Phil my drink for me, will you?

Knock, knock!
Who's there?
Senior!
Senior who?
Senior so nosy, I'm not going to tell you who it is!

Knock, knock!
Who's there?
Leaf!
Leaf who?
Leaf me alone with all your silly questions!

Knock, knock!
Who's there?
Burton!
Burton who?
Burton me are going fishing, want to come?

Knock, knock!
Who's there?
Lion!
Lion who?
Lion down on the job will get you fired!

Knock, knock!
Who's there?
Iguana!
Iguana who?
Iguana hold your hand!

Knock, knock!
Who's there?
Hayden!
Hayden who?
Hayden won't do any good, I can see you through the mail slot!

Knock, knock!
Who's there?
Isis!
Isis who?
Isis giving me a brain freeze!

Knock, knock!
Who's there?
Izzy!
Izzy who?
Izzy coming out to play, or do I have to stand here all day?

Knock, knock!
Who's there?
Cello!
Cello who?
Cello there, my little friend. How are you?

Knock, knock!
Who's there?
Dennis!
Dennis who?
Dennis is my favorite game!

SILLY JOKES

What do you get when you cross a bell with a bee?

A humdinger!

What kind of ship did Dracula captain?

A blood vessel!

Who wears long underwear and glitters?

Long John Silver!

What did one toe say to the other toe?

"Don't look now, but there are a couple of heels following us!"

What moves around a bus at 1,000 mph?
A lightning conductor!

What do you do with a sick wasp?

Take it to the waspital!

What do you get when you pour hot water down rabbit holes?

Hot cross bunnies!

What is brown, hairy, and limps?

A coconut with blisters!

What do policemen say to men with three heads?

"Hello. Hello. Hello!"

What shows do ghosts like best at the theater?

Phantomines!

Who was Noah's wife?

Joan of Ark!

Why was the sheep arrested on the highway?

It made a ewe turn!

What is brown, has four legs, and can see as well from either end?

A horse with its eyes shut!

What is the best cure for flat feet?

A foot pump!

What is a British scientist's favorite food?

Fission chips!

What is essential for deaf fishermen?

A herring aid!

Wacky Wizardry

What do little witches call art day at school?

Witch craft day!

What was wrong with the forgetful wizard's memory?

It had a tendency to wand-er!

What did the wizard say to his girlfriend before the dance?

"My dear, you look wand-erful!"

What dance did the wizard take the witch to?

The Crystal Ball!

What did the wizard say to the vampire when he knew he was wrong?

"Sorry, it was a mis-stake!"

Why did the wizard send his friend an hourglass in the mail?

He wanted to see time travel!

What did the wizard's friend say after he turned him into an antelope?

"That's gnus to me!"

How do witches know how much money you have?

Because they know how to tell your fortune!

What do wizards use to
open haunted houses?

A spoooo-key!

Why do wizards love to eat at
family restaurants?

**Because they have the
biggest potions!**

Why don't wizards like to
cast spells on boats?

They get potion sickness!

Why was the little wizard angry
at his big sister?

**Because she was always
potion him around!**

What did the old wizard say to his
frustrated pupil?

**"Stay calm, my son.
Potions is a virtue!"**

Why don't wizards need glasses?

Because they have eye of newt!

What did the wizard say to the spirit of
the gambling man?

**"You don't have a ghost
of a chance!"**

Why are ghosts vegetarians?

**Because they don't like to
haunt animals!**

COMIC CRITTERS

What do you call a bear with no shoes?

Bear-foot!

What do you call a duck that steals?

A robber ducky!

What did the mother kangaroo give birth to?

A bouncing baby!

What do you call the place where desert animals rest?

Camel lot!

What can you call a camel without a hump?

Humphrey! (hump-free)

Why do tigers eat raw meat?

Because they're bad cooks!

What does a skunk buy for its home-entertainment system?

Smell-o-vision!

Why are skunks so dumb?

They never use good scents!

What do you call a monkey that has just turned seven?

A birthday baboon! (balloon)

Why do wolves have fur coats?

Because they would be cold wearing just hats!

What ape is a real pal?

A chum-panzee!

How do you stop a wild boar from charging?

Take away its credit card!

What kind of bike does a polar bear ride?

An ice-cycle!

Why are elephants so cheap?

The get paid peanuts!

UNDER WHERE?

What kind of underwear does Muhammad Ali wear?

Boxers, of course!

What kind of swimsuits do pelicans wear?

Beak-inies!

What did the swimmer say about the little bikini?

"It was itsy-bitsy teenie-weenie!"

What do you call the money you use to buy underwear?

Shortbread!

How did the woman in the swimsuit feel after escaping from a shark?

She felt lucky to be in a one-piece!

What is the fastest swimsuit around?

The Speedo!

What did the sunbather have after falling asleep in his Speedo?

Hot crossed buns!

Why did the fast swimmer have to pull out of the race?

He got pulled over for Speedo-ing!

What kind of underwear do New York basketball players wear?

Knick-ers!

What did the woman call her fun, fancy underwear?

Her silly frillies!

What kind of underwear do baseball players wear?

Short stops!

Knock, knock!
Who's there?
C-2!
C-2 who?
C-2 it that you don't forget to wear your underwear!

What do you call old underwear?

Behind the times!

What do you call a snake that wears diapers?

A diaper viper!

Why won't Ron wear white underwear?

Because you can't white a Ron!

Where do you keep your shorts when you travel?

In your briefcase!

XTREME-LY FUNNY

Why do snowboarders make such bad farmers?

Because they hate to bale! (bail)

How do the snorkelers know when it's dinnertime?

They hear the diving bell!

What do divers use to take photos under the water?

A fish-eye lens, of course!

Why did the surfer cross the water?

To get to the other tide!

What was the saddest animal the diver had ever seen?

The blue whale!

What do skaters like that boxers hate?

A fat lip!

What does one wear to a surfer's wedding?

A good wet suit!

What kind of music do deep-sea divers love?

Sole music!

When should you never let a BMXer stay over at your house?

When she asks if she can crash on your couch!

What is a BMXer's worst enemy?

Gravity!

Why are boarders such dreamers?

Because they never want to come back down to earth!

What is the worst thing you can say to an in-line trick skater?

"You're grounded!"

Why are surfers great gamblers?

Because they know when to let it ride!

What do skaters have in common with Fred Flintstone?

They all like to go bowling!

Knock, knock!
Who's there?
Indy!
Indy who?
Indy mood to go surfing?

What is it called when a wave is so big that a surfer doesn't stop until he hits the grass?

Surf and turf!

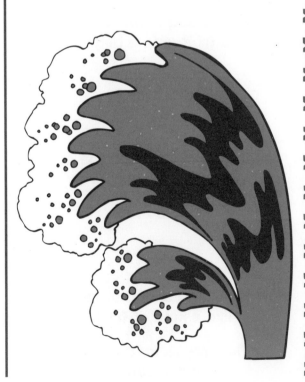

CAFETERIA COMEDY

What fruit question is on the cafeteria menu?

What are melons? (watermelons)

What is the sad result of crossing a fruit with a dog?

Melon-collie!

What kind of fruit did the cook use to fix her flat tire?

A pump-kin!

How is holding a kind of rock just like a kind of fruit?

When you palm a granite! (pomegranate)

How did the cheese feel after the cook shredded it?

It was grate-full!

Where do baby cows go to eat lunch?

The calf-a-teria!

Where do cafeteria cooks go to prepare the potatoes?

To the mush-room!

What is golden soup made of?

Fourteen carrots! (carats)

What vegetable's easiest recipe is the same as its name?

Squash!

What is the opposite of spaghetti?

Antipasto!

What is the worst thing about eating in the cafeteria?

The food, of course!

Who loves cafeteria food?

Bugs!

What is a tree's favorite soft drink?

Root beer!

What did the cook say to a sulky grape?

"Quit your wining!"

SILLY SPIES

What is a young spy's favorite
TV show?

Blue's Clues!

What did the spy say when his
canine companion defected?

"Dog-gone it!"

What did the undercover agent
name his dog?

Snoop-y!

Why was the sniffing spy dog so full
of duty?

*Because it knew what it had been
scent to do!*

Why did the secret agent think that
his dog was a spy?

*Because he caught it sniffing
around!*

What did the detective say to the
spy dog?

"Please stop hounding me!"

What happened when the spy's dog
lost the scent?

It got into a real furry flurry!

What did the spy dog say about
sneaking around?

*"It's a ruff job, but somebody's got
to do it!"*

Why did the spy dog like to be taken for a walk?

Because it knew that it would have a good lead!

What did the spy kitten want to be when it grew up?

A cat burglar!

Why do cats make good spies?

Because they know how to prowl!

What do you call the canine unit of the Secret Service?

The Federal Beagle of Investigation!

Where did the feline spy keep its gear?

In a tool kit-ten!

KNOCK, KNOCK!

Knock, knock!
Who's there?
Sara!
Sara who?
*Sara nother question
you could ask me?*

Knock, knock!
Who's there?
Ken!
Ken who?
**Ken I come in, or are you gonna
leave me out here all day?**

Knock, knock!
Who's there?
Ollie!
Ollie who?
**Ollie said was that I should
come visit you!**

Knock, knock!
Who's there?
Rufus!
Rufus who?
*Rufus leaking. You'd better
get it fixed!*

Knock, knock!
Who's there?
Don Juan!
Don Juan who?
**Don Juan to go to school today.
It's too nice outside!**

Knock, knock!
Who's there?
Shane!
Shane who?
**Shane on you! You don't
recognize your own brother!**

Knock, knock!
Who's there?
Wade!
Wade who?
**Wade till I get inside,
then I'll tell you!**

Knock, knock!
Who's there?
Tex!
Tex who?
Tex one to know one!

Knock, knock!
Who's there?
Lisa!
Lisa who?
**Lisa you can do is let me in!
It's pouring rain!**

Knock, knock!
Who's there?
Alfie!
Alfie who?
Alfie crying out loud, stop asking!

Knock, knock!
Who's there?
Simon!
Simon who?
**Simon the other side of the door. If
you opened it, you'd know!**

SILLY JOKES

What do nostalgic vampires sing?

"Fangs for the memory."

What would the Swiss be without all those mountains?

Alp-less!

Hear about the musical thief?

He got away with the lute!

How do you find out where a flea has bitten you?

You start from scratch!

What is wild, German, and lays eggs?

Attila the Hen!

Hear about the boxing canary?

He was a featherweight champion!

How about the author who made a fortune?

He was in the write business!

Who is a vampire's favorite composer?

Bathoven!

What is big, gray, and mutters?

A mumbo jumbo!

Why do devils and ghosts get along very well?

Because demons are a ghoul's best friend!

What happens when you cross a hen with a poodle?

You get pooched eggs!

How do you get through life with only one tooth?

You grin and bear it!

Why does Dracula love to go to the races?

He loves to bat on the horses!

What has four legs, is green, and is deadly when it jumps at you?

An angry billiard table!

Why do vampires brush their teeth regularly?

To avoid bat breath!

Wacky Wizardry

How do wizards guarantee peace?

They get a warlock!

What do little warlocks love on their nachos?

Cheese wiz!

Who is the most famous wiz of all?

Oz just about to ask you that!

What do wizards call phony spells?

Hocus bogus!

What did the wizard say after the fishing accident?

"Help! Hook-has poke-us!"

What do wizards say to their young students who can't concentrate?

"Hocus focus!"

What do you say to a wizard who is a daydreamer?

"Wish not, wand not!"

What does a wizard say when he gets to his front door?

"Open says me!"

What did the wizard say after he lost a game of chess to the little sprite?

"Fairy 'nuff!"

What did the wizard say to the lazy monster?

"Quit dragon your tail!"

What do wizards think of little, flying people?

That they're fairy interesting!

What did the wizard say to the little girl who wanted to study magic?

"Witching you the best of luck!"

Where did the wizard meet his elf friend for their fishing trip?

Down at the dwarf!

What did the wizard say when his little sidekick went away on vacation?

"I feel so elfless!"

Why can't babies do magic?

Because they don't know how to spell!

What did the wizard say when he was buying the elf's walking stick?

"Gnome your price!"

UNDER WHERE?

What kind of underwear do horses wear?

Jockeys!

What kind of jumps do jockeys do?

Girdle hurdles!

Why did the woman keep checking her pantyhose drawer?

Because she needed to take stocking!

What do you call it when Santa checks his inventory?

Christmas stocking!

What kind of socks do horn players wear?

Tuba socks!

What kind of underwear do comedians wear?

Joke-ys!

Why did the underwear keep moving around?

Because it was jockeying for position!

What kind of underwear
fits over a shell?

A turtle girdle!

What did the boxer shorts
say to the pantyhose?

"Sock it to me!"

What kind of shirt do generals wear
under their suits?

Tank tops, of course!

*Knock, knock!
Who's there?
Handel!
Handel who?
Handel your underwear
with care!*

Where do pantyhose go
to meet stockings?

To a sock hop!

How do you cover up your foot?

You socket!

What do chickens wear
under their pants?

Hen-derwear!

Why do stockings always feel safe?

*Because they've got a garter!
(guarder)*

What kind of socks
do firefighters wear?

Fire hose!

XTREME-LY FUNNY

How do you train for
the big wave?

Practice rip curls!

How do extreme surfers greet each
other?

Hey, Haw-ai-i?

What is the one hairstyle surfers
don't mind having?

A permanent wave!

What do extreme ski jumpers love
most about their car stereos?

The aerials!

Why were the surfers happy to hear
that a storm was coming?

*Because they thought it was a
wind-wind situation!*

Why didn't the man use his new
cross-country skis?

*He was searching for a very small
country!*

How did the reckless skier get rid of
her extra gear?

She had a yard sale!

Knock, knock!
Who's there?
Ida!
Ida who?
*Ida like to learn how to
ride a BMX bike!*

How did the extreme jumper show that he was excited?

He flipped out!

Why didn't the musician board on the big hill?

She was afraid that she'd B flat!

How did the bummed-out boarder pick himself up?

He got on the chair lift!

When you take the big jump, what are your rhyming choices mid-air?

Sail or bail!

Who won when the climbers raced to make the quickest knot?

It was a tie!

Why was the climbing movie split into two parts?

Because it was a cliff-hanger!

How did the surfer feel after a whole weekend on the sunny sea?

Burned out!

How did the diver's trip go?

Swimmingly!

KNOCK, KNOCK!

Knock, knock!
Who's there?
Little old lady!
Little old lady who?
I didn't know you could yodel!

Knock, knock!
Who's there?
Cassidy!
Cassidy who?
*Cassidy was going to be right back.
Is he home?*

Knock, knock!
Who's there?
Sam!
Sam who?
Sam day, you'll remember.

Knock, knock!
Who's there?
Zoe!
Zoe who?
*Zoe doesn't recognize my
voice now?*

Knock, knock!
Who's there?
Maya!
Maya who?
*Maya foot seems to be a caught
in your door!*

Knock, knock!
Who's there?
Yuri!
Yuri who?
Yuri up and open the door!

Knock, knock!
Who's there?
Mabel!
Mabel who?
*Mabel syrup is good on
waffles!*

Knock, knock!
Who's there?
Ach!
Ach who?
Gesundheit!

Knock, knock!
Who's there?
Klaus!
Klaus who?
Klaus the window, I can hear
your television all the way down
the street!

Knock, knock!
Who's there?
Deecha!
Deecha who?
Deecha miss me while I
was gone?

Knock, knock!
Who's there?
Thermos!
Thermos who?
Thermos be some way out
of here!

Knock, knock!
Who's there?
Colleen!
Colleen who?
Colleen all cars! Colleen all cars!
We have a knock-knock joke
in progress!

 SILLY SPIES

Why did the scuba-diving agent feel so low?

Because she had a sinking feeling!

Why did the spy find on the ship?

What happened to the scuba-diving spy?

He tanked!

Why didn't the spy want to dive to the sunken sub?

He couldn't handle the pressure!

What do deep-sea spies have for lunch?

Subs!

Where was the scuba-diving spy afraid to swim?

In the Dead Sea!

What did the spy find on the ship?

A conspira-sea!

Why didn't anybody believe the scuba-diving spy?

Because she had no ground to stand on!

Why did the scuba-diving spy hate it when his phone rang under water?

Because it left a wringing in his ears!

What did the secret agent do when he got on board the boat?

He performed a ship-search!

What do you call an underwater secret agent?

James Pond!

Where do spies go when they die?

To double-oh-heaven!

How can spy submarines see so well?

Because they're made for deep-sea vision!

What should every sloppy spy have?

A license to spill!

What did the spy call the fishy dealer?

A card shark!

SILLY JOKES

What do you call a pig who tells long, dull stories?

A big boar, of course!

Why did the princess fall in love with the taxi?

Because it was a very handsome cab! (hansom cab)

What did the big flower say to the little flower?

"How are you, bud?"

Why was the baker so lazy?

He did nothing but loaf!

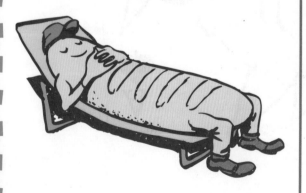

Why do elephants paint their toenails red?

So they can hide in cherry trees!

Why do people carry umbrellas?

Because umbrellas can't walk!

Why didn't the coffee cake have many friends?

It was crumby!

What was the baker's favorite dance?

The twist!

Why is the baker so rich?

He makes a lot of dough!

How do you get four elephants into a compact car?

Two in the front and two in the back!

How do you get four giraffes into the same compact car?

You can't until you get those elephants out!

Where do sugar fairies live?

Gnome sweet gnome!

What do you call a mischievous egg?

A practical yolk!

Who is short, afraid of wolves, and shouts a lot?

Little Rude Riding Hood!

What do you call a cat that sucks lemons?

A sour puss!

Who has huge antlers and wears white gloves?

Mickey Moose!

Wacky Wizardry

What do American fairies sing at the beginning of every baseball game?

Stars and Sprites!

Why do wizards make good friends?

Because they're charming!

How are wizards' books held together?

They're spellbound!

What is it called when wizards get together and sing without instruments?

Acca-spell-a! (a cappella)

Where do witches go when they run out of eye of newt and tongue of frog?

To the gross-ery store!

What do speedy monsters love to do most?

Dragon racing!

What did the elf say when he was tired of Oz?

"There's no place like gnome!"

Why do witches chew gum?

Because they're afraid of having bat breath!

What do wizards call their magic books?

The Go-spell!

What is the name of the richest American wizard?

Rocka-spell-a! (Rockefeller)

Why did the witch decide to get a new broom?

She wanted to make a clean sweep of it!

Why did the witch need to practice with her new broom?

Because she needed to brush up on her flying!

Why do witches fly to their secret caves?

Because it's too far to walk!

What did the wizard's kitten say before his magic trick?

"Abra cat-abra!"

What did the pirate want the witch to find for him?

Sleeping booty!

Knock, knock!
Who's there?
Witches!
Witches who?
Witches to put a spell on you!

# CAFETERIA COMEDY

What do the geeks eat in the cafeteria?

Square meals!

Why should you go to the cafeteria before computer class?

To have a little byte!

Why did the boy swallow the dollar bill?

His parents told him it was his lunch money!

When are students like pigs?

When they eat the slop at the cafeteria!

What do you say when you find a dead bug in your soup at school?

"He must have tasted it!"

What did one cook say to the other when they went on vacation?

"Meat me in St. Louis!"

How do you know when it's time to eat at the cafeteria?

When they lock the doors behind you!

What did the student from France say after eating lunch at the cafeteria?

"Mercy!" (merci)

What is the difference between the school cafeteria's meat loaf and bricks?

Not much!

Why was the student looking at her lunch with a magnifying glass?

She was trying to solve the mystery meat!

What do you call something that is brown and sticky in your food at the cafeteria?

A stick!

When there is only one thing on the menu at school, how come you still have a choice?

You can choose not to eat it!

Why did the girl think that she had chicken pox?

Because the chicken she had at the cafeteria was a little spotty!

How do you know lunch is over at the cafeteria?

By all the moaning!

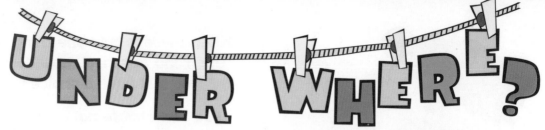

UNDER WHERE?

What do you call a shirt that Sir Lancelot wears to sleep?

A knight shirt!

What is a clean pair of stockings' favorite sports team?

The Chicago White Sox, of course!

Knock, knock!
Who's there?
Warren!
Warren who?
I'm Warren my favorite pair of underwear!

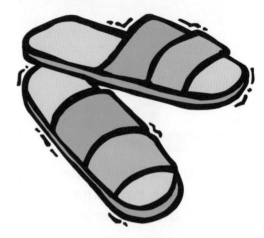

What do you call indoor shoes that help you slide?

House slippers!

What are the best initials for comfy sleeping?

P.J.!

What do you call bright yellow PJs?

Banana pajamas!

What do you call PJs that are too small?

Tighty nighties!

What kind of underwear does a home wear?

A housecoat!

What do you call shoes that you wear to bed?

Sleeper slippers!

What do you call a housecoat that you wear to make a salad?

A dressing gown!

What do you call women's shorts that are always behind?

Fanny!

What does the postman wear on his feet at night?

Shipper slippers!

What do you call it when you throw out the top of your underwear?

Waste-band! (waistband)

What do underwear like to read?

Boxer short stories!

What do you call it when you quickly alter your long underwear?

A short cut!

What does the green-thumbed woman wear on her legs?

Garden hose!

XTREME-LY FUNNY

What did the in-line skater say after crashing down the hill?

"Give me a brake!"

Knock, knock!
Who's there?
Claire!
Claire who?
Claire the way, I'm coming down the hill!

What do you call an in-line skater who crashes and burns?

A trailblazer!

What part of the in-line skate can you never trust?

The heel!

How do you say good-bye to an in-line fanatic?

"Later, skater!"

What did the in-line skater say when she got lost in the skate shop?

"I can't seem to get my bearings!"

What is the in-line skater's motto?

Roll with it!

How did the boarder make the hill angry?

He just kept crossing it!

What did the in-line skater say to his buddy when he saw dogs chasing them?

"Don't look now, but I think we're being tailed!"

What is the worst part about racing downhill against the clock?

The time is always running down!

Why do in-line skates seem so rude?

Because they always stick out their tongues!

What do you get when you rewind your skate-tricks video?

Some wicked backslides!

What do boarders have in common with martial artists?

They both love the kick flip!

What do boarders have in common with the big rig riders?

They all love their trucks!

What did the boarders say when they were playing hide and seek?

"Ollie, Ollie, oxen free!"

What did the dentist say to the skater?

"I want you to stop grinding your teeth!"

KNOCK, KNOCK!

Knock, knock!
Who's there?
Boo!
Boo who?
There, there, don't cry.

Knock, knock!
Who's there?
Paul!
Paul who?
Paul up a chair, and I'll tell you!

Knock, knock!
Who's there?
Sandy!
Sandy who?
**Sandy beaches beat snowstorms
any day!**

Knock, knock!
Who's there?
Max!
Max who?
**Max no difference if you let me in
or not! I can wait all day!**

Knock, knock!
Who's there?
Daryl!
Daryl who?
**Daryl never be another girl
like you!**

Knock, knock!
Who's there?
Mary!
Mary who?
Mary me, why don't ya?

Knock, knock!
Who's there?
Tom Sawyer!
Tom Sawyer who?
Tom Sawyer paint job on his fence. Boy are you in trouble!

Knock, knock!
Who's there?
Simon!
Simon who?
Simon the dotted line and all your troubles will be over!

Knock, knock!
Who's there?
Water!
Water who?
Water you waiting for? Open up!

Knock, knock!
Who's there?
Tony!
Tony who?
Tony even know me anymore?

Knock, knock!
Who's there?
Sweden!
Sweden who?
Sweden sour chicken is yummy!

Knock, knock!
Who's there?
Augusta!
Augusta who?
Augusta wind is coming your way!

SILLY JOKES

What goes "Dit-dit-dot bzzz" and then bites you?

A morsequito!

Who wrote Great Eggspectations?

Charles Chickens!

What is bright yellow, weighs a ton, has four legs, and sings?

Two half-ton canaries!

Why do bears have fur coats?

Because they would look silly in raincoats!

What do ghosts have for breakfast?

Dreaded wheat!

Why do insects hum?

Because they don't know the words!

What do vampires take for a bad cold?

Coffin drops!

What happens when you cross a Jeep with a pet dog?

You get a land rover!

It's sad about the human cannonball at the circus.

He got fired!

What animal hibernates standing on its head?

Yoga Bear!

What is green, knobby, and writes essays?

A ball-point pickle!

Hear about the burglars who stole a calendar?

They each got six months!

What did one raisin say to the other raisin?

Nothing. Raisins can't talk!

Who couldn't get their airplane to fly?

The wrong brothers!

What do you need to get back runaway rabbits?

Hare restorer!

Pet Punchlines

How do cats stop their favorite videos?

They put them on paws! (pause)

What did the cat say after it caught the rat?

"Sorry, my mouse-stake!"

What kind of feline can you never trust?

A copycat!

What do you get when you cross a cat and a fish?

A purr-anha!

Why shouldn't you keep a piranha as a pet?

Because it has a fish's temper!

What kind of dogs always get into fights?

Boxers!

What happened to the teddy bear that got into a fight with a dog?

He got the stuffing knocked out of him!

What kind of pet always has a sore throat?

A hoarse!

What does your cat like on hot days?

Mice cubes!

What did one cat say to the other after it saw that they were being followed by a dog?

"Don't look now, but I think we're being tailed!"

How do you reward a horse that pulls your carriage on your wedding day?

With a bridle sweet!

Which dog makes the most boring pet?

The poo-dull!

What do you feed a cat that yowls all night long?

Tune-a-fish!

Which side of a dog has the most hair?

The outside!

 SILLY SPIES

What did the spy say to his friend who was hiding behind the curtain?

"Pull yourself together!"

What did the secret agent say to the camping spy?

"You're so tents!"

Why did the spy hate to play cards at the casino?

Because she found them hard to deal with!

Why did the detective think that snooping around an apple farm would help him solve the case?

He thought he would get to the core of it!

What did the spy say after she got poison ivy from spying in the bushes?

"I made a rash decision!"

What did the spy think about having to drill peepholes in a wall all day?

That it was really boring!

Why didn't the spy want to look for clues in the trash?

Because he thought it was a waste of time!

Why did the spy think the forgery ring was hilarious?

Because of all the funny money!

☞☜

What did the martial-arts spy drink in the afternoon?

Kara-tea!

☞☜

What did the spy think after he was bitten by mosquitoes in the swamp?

That he was a sucker for taking the job!

☞☜

What did the spy say about his enemy who got out of the cheese factory?

"He made a grate escape!"

Why wasn't the spy surprised that his enemy wanted to lower him into boiling oil?

Because it was Fry-day!

☞☜

How did the spy feel when the enemy agent stole his shoes?

De-feeted!

☞☜

Why did the spy put a banana peel in front of his closet?

So he could slip into something more comfortable!

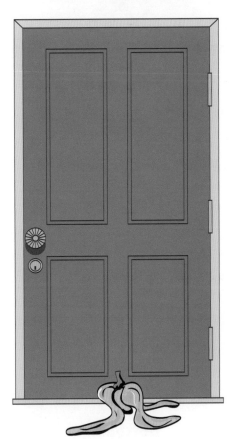

Wacky Wizardry

Knock, knock!
Who's there?
Wiz!
Wiz who?
Wiz a matter, you don't recognize me?

If you spin around and around, what kind of magic will you create?

A dizzy spell!

What kind of spell makes you thirsty?

A dry spell!

What is a witch's favorite pet?

A wart hog!

Who is a witch's favorite musician?

Bats Domino!

What is a vampire's favorite sport?

Batsball!

Why are magicians such fast readers?

Because they know how to wiz through a good book!

Why don't vampires change into pelicans?

Because pelicans are too big to fly in through bedroom windows!

What is a wizard's favorite cereal?

Lucky Charms!

What do you call the most powerful
wizard of all?

Whatever he wants you to!

What do you call a female wizard
at the beach?

A sandy-witch!

What do you call a criminal elf?

A lepre-con!

What do Eskimo leprechauns keep
at the end of the rainbow?

A lucky pot of cold!

What do you call a leprechaun's dog?

A four-leafed Rover!

What did the Bigfoot put in his garden?

Sas-squash!

How do wizards roast their
marshmallows?

With dragon's breath!

COMIC CRITTERS

What do you call a greasy pachyderm?

An oily-phant!

Why was Billy so mad?

Somebody got his goat!

How do rabbits toast each other?

"Hare's to you!"

What did the big buffalo say as the little buffalo left for school?

"Bison!" ("Bye, son!")

What is the best prison for a criminal deer?

Elk-a-traz! (Alcatraz)

Where do big cats go when they're sick?

To leopard (leper) colonies!

What do you call a battle between the big cats of the wild?

A jag war! (jaguar)

How do lions do their shopping?

From cat-alogues!

Why don't snakes need eating utensils?

Because they have forked tongues!